To Donna

From: Denny, Carol
+ Andy

Happy Easter 2002

When Life Throws You a Curveball, Hit It

Simple Wisdom for Life's Ups & Downs

by
Criswell Freeman, Psy. D.

WALNUT GROVE PRESS
Nashville, TN 37211

Library of Congress Catalog Card Number 94-66136

ISBN 1-58334-002-5

Printed in the United States of America
Cover: Tal Howell
Typesetting & Page Layout: Sue Gerdes
2 3 4 5 6 7 8 9 10 • 99 00 01 02 03 04

ACKNOWLEDGMENTS
The author gratefully acknowledges the love and support of Angela Freeman and
Dick and Mary Freeman.

For Mary Susan
and
All of My Business Associates

Who Courageously Took Their Swings

Table of Contents

Introduction

Albert Einstein once said, "Make everything as simple as possible, but not simpler." With this thought in mind, I have written a book about the psychology of tough times. My interest in this topic springs not only from extensive training in the field of psychology but also from personal experience.

By the time I was 35, I had achieved success as the world measures it. I headed a company that was among the largest residential landlords in America. I owned a piece of the American dream, complete with a big house, a corporate airplane, and a mountain cabin.

In the late 1980's, on the heels of a severely depressed real estate market, I experienced a financial setback that left me breathless. Eventually, I awoke to the realization that I must start over from scratch. Such was my personal introduction to tough times.

After much thought, I decided to embark upon a totally new career: psychology. I entered graduate school in Chicago and earned my doctorate, all the while gathering information for this text. In its original form, this book was longer and more technical in nature. It contained many psychological buzz words, impressive terminology, and plenty of advice. But as I read and re-read the manuscript, I remembered how I had felt during my own hard times. I remembered that I didn't have the energy to wade through technicalities; I remembered that I didn't want theories. What I wanted and needed were practical solutions. And I needed to hear them from someone who had been there.

This is the book I wish I could have read during my own difficult times. I make no apologies for the uncomplicated nature of its message. Tough times cry out for solutions that are "as simple as possible, but not simpler." These essays, simple though they may be, contain powerful solutions that are espoused by mental health professionals from a variety of disciplines.

I am particularly indebted to Alfred Adler and his followers, to the cognitive-behavioral psychologists, to the Existential movement and to Glasser's Reality Therapy. Casual readers may have little interest in the ways that these theories are woven through my stories, but they may be comforted to know that the ideas have been distilled from decades of study and research. I am also indebted to my editor, Angela Beasley Freeman, who helped me condense this message into 18 brief essays.

If life has tossed you a curveball, this book was written with you in mind. It is my sincere hope that you will find the following stories and concepts helpful. Whatever you do, don't despair and don't give up. Simply keep reading, keep your spirits up, and above all, keep swinging. Your persistence and your courage will be rewarded.

When Life Throws
You a Curveball,
Hit It

*Courage is resistance
to fear, mastery of fear —
not absence of fear.*

Mark Twain
1835 - 1910

As a kid, I played baseball in the Junior Knot Hole League. This was Nashville's version of the Little League, complete with uniforms, organized teams, and volunteer coaches. I can still recall the dusty fields, the sliding pads, and the uncomfortable, spiked shoes. I can still remember the coaches' faces, the names of my teammates and the positions everyone played. But the single-most unforgettable moment in my baseball career was my first encounter with a curveball pitcher.

Please understand the impact of a curveball on a ten-year-old. This pitch bends as it approaches the plate, making it difficult to hit. Fastballs are tough enough, but curveballs? Forget it. Curveballs are murder.

Enter Ed White.

Ed White was the most feared pitcher in the Junior Knot Hole League, because he possessed a smoking fastball and a nasty curve. Ed's reputation for toughness clearly established him as the best player in town. My teammates and I dreaded the day we would face the juggernaut White, but that day arrived, and we found ourselves staring down the barrel of a loaded arm.

The first time I batted against Ed, I nearly jumped out of my cleats. His fastball had lots of zing, but I had seen fastballs before; fastballs didn't scare me — much. Curveballs were different. A curveball was an unknown, dangerous phenomenon.

It's no surprise that my introduction to Ed White's curveball was a terrifying experience. And it's no surprise that I secretly wanted to turn in my uniform. But, with friends and parents watching, I was more fearful of quitting than batting, so I stepped up to the plate, quietly trembling.

As White began his windup, the butterflies in my stomach felt like eagles. Ed pitched and I flinched. Three pitches later, it was all over: I struck out, and I was not alone. My teammates and I spent the entire game dancing away from pitch after pitch; we couldn't hit the ball because our fears got in the way.

Only years later did I learn that a curveball is relatively easy to hit — under the right circumstances. A curve isn't as speedy as a fastball, and sometimes it doesn't break as much as the pitcher intends. A batter with skill and patience can hit curveballs as easily as other pitches, but he can't hit them while he's jumping out of the batter's box. Instead, he's got to stand up and face the pitch, like it or not.

Life is like Ed White. It is very good at throwing curveballs. While you're hoping for a straight pitch right over the plate, it's seldom that easy. Just when you think you have things figured out, the unexpected happens. Your life is proceeding along just fine, and then — out of the blue — something goes wrong. Trouble arrives, ties your stomach in knots, and leaves you wondering if you'll ever get another hit.

Welcome to tough times.

Tough times come in all shapes and sizes: divorce, financial strain, job loss or ill health, to name just a few. When life takes a turn for the worse (as it must from time to time), you may be tempted to give up in disgust and turn in your uniform. Not so fast. Maybe you don't need to quit — maybe you simply need to learn a little bit more about hitting curveballs.

This book is about hitting life's tough pitches. It's about overcoming problems and facing fears. It is about controlling emotions rather than allowing emotions to control you. It is about confronting reality and getting on with the important business of living.

You may be under the mistaken belief that your problems are simply too complicated. You may feel your situation is so unique and so difficult that you'll never find a way out. If so, you are mistaken. Your problems may be severe, but they are not unique, and they are not without solution. In fact, the lessons you'll need for overcoming personal adversity are simple ones — simple reminders of principles you learned many years ago. This book is intended to serve as a gentle reminder of those lessons.

What is the secret for hitting life's difficult pitches? To become a good curveball hitter — on or off the baseball diamond — you need *knowledge*, *courage*, and *patience*.

Your knowledge comes as you learn and live through tough times. Talking with informed people helps. So do books like this one. Whatever your problem, knowledge is power, so it's up to you to learn as much as you can about your situation and about yourself.

You exhibit courage by standing at the plate

and giving it your best effort, even when you are afraid. But beware: If you are like most of us, your first inclination will be to withdraw from the game.

All of us, from time to time, are reluctant batters. We become paralyzed by our discomforts so we do nothing, hoping that our problems will take care of themselves. Regrettably, most problems are not self-solving. That's why we need to act courageously, even when we'd rather run away.

Courage is the ability to take action when action is difficult; it is the ability to face a situation head-on and do the thing that needs doing — when it needs doing — even when we'd rather be doing something else. Courage is an indispensable currency during tough times, because it frees us from the quicksand of inaction and allows us to solve our problems rather than avoid them.

If the problems you face can be solved by quick, decisive action (and a surprising number of situations fit this description), then you must, at all costs, avoid the temptation to do nothing. Instead, you must step back up to the plate. The quicker you begin swinging, and the more swings you take, the sooner you'll begin working yourself out of trouble. But don't expect to become a great curveball hitter overnight.

When tough times arrive, they usually overstay their welcome, so you will need patience. In this case, patience is defined as an ability to retain an optimistic attitude despite the absence of immediate positive feedback. A patient attitude is an invaluable asset during tough times, because it allows you to continue working long after other, less mature individuals would have tossed in the towel.

As you work persistently, expect gradual improvement — not instant gratification. Remember that on this journey, as on every journey, direction is more important than speed.

If you are having trouble hitting the pitches life has tossed your way, or if you know someone who is, read on. The first time that you face that daunting curveball, you may flinch — you may even strike out. But with a little knowledge, a lot of courage, and some patience, you can hit like a star. If that sounds appealing, turn the page.

And bring on Ed White.

The Miracle of Your Mind

*A mind enlightened
is like heaven;
a mind in darkness
is like hell.*

Chinese Proverb

Take a moment to consider the miraculous powers of the most complicated creation on earth: the human brain. Composed of trillions of separate yet interconnected cells, your brain allows you to live, breathe, think, hope, and dream.

As you view the words on this page, your heart continues to beat, your blood pressure and temperature are regulated, and a multitude of internal organs sustain your bodily functions. Your eyes focus and refocus as you read; without thinking, you hold the book in place. In addition, you have enough spare brain power to think about the words you are reading.

Issued to you free of charge at birth, your brain never takes a vacation, never goes on strike and never shuts itself off. Even while you sleep, it keeps working, never stopping for a single moment. Though your brain contains trillions of moving parts, it's never closed for repairs — it just keeps doing the job, day after day, month after month, year after year.

Over a lifetime, you and your environment continue to transform your brain into something even more miraculous: a mind. What results is your own unique personality, one that is different from any other living human — past or present. Your mind has the potential to become a high-powered tool for good, an invaluable personal resource with almost unlimited problem-solving ability.

You are the sole owner of this highly creative problem-solving machine. Possibly, you've been taking all this power for granted. If so, it's time to reconsider. You have at your disposal a powerful tool for solving your dilemma: a human brain. This brain will be your best friend or your worst enemy, depending upon how you use it.

Given the brain's great potential, one thing seems clear:

Your mind is more powerful than your problems.

If you use your mental capacities effectively, you can perform miracles. What's required is clear thinking, realistic expectations and a positive outlook.

But, just as your mind can be a wonderful tool for good, it can also become a self-imposed torture chamber. Tough times have a way of distorting your thoughts. Once your mind starts rolling down the highway of gloom, it quickly picks up speed. Soon, your problems seem hopeless, because you've allowed the power of your mind to work against your own best interests. Left unchecked, irrational, negative thoughts will make you miserable and cause you physical harm. If that weren't enough, needless worry also inhibits your ability to solve problems.

Ironically, the more you worry about your troubles, the less likely you are to find solutions. You're simply too distraught to be effective. So instead of agonizing over your problems, convert that brain-power into productive thought. Here's how:

First, understand that most worries result from irrational, exaggerated thinking. As humans, we're programmed to make mountains out of molehills. All of us do this from time to time; we possess the ability to imagine the worst and then worry about it. Most of our fears never come to pass, but we worry about them with so much gusto that we pay a terrible price: needless, paralyzing anxiety.

Fretting over problems rather than solving them is unproductive human behavior — the price we pay for anticipating future events. Your challenge is simple: Understand that most of your worries, especially those about far-off future events, are greatly exaggerated.

Second, it is important to understand that much of your psychological distress results from your own unrealistic desire for things to occur *exactly* as you hope they will occur. You're probably telling yourself that events "must" unfold in a certain way, that you "must" look good, or that you "must" achieve the outcome you seek. Your desires, though common, are unrealistic. If you're expecting life to conform to your every wish, it's time for a healthy dose of flexibility coupled with a heaping helping of reality. Try decreasing your demands upon life, and watch your worries fade away.

Third, it is important to realize that your fears are being amplified by your own anxiety. Once you begin to worry about a particular situation, your emotions tend to snowball. Before you consciously realize what has happened, you have become caught up in an uncomfortable, emotional frenzy. Your task is straightforward:

When irrational fears arise, catch yourself in the act of worrying and then interrupt the process before it gets out of hand. Take a few deep breaths. Quiet yourself, and regain the natural calm that will allow you to think more clearly.

In overcoming irrational beliefs, you will find it helpful to examine the negative messages that you send yourself, and discover the exaggerations that hide behind them. Then have an honest talk with yourself and put things back into proper perspective.

Sometimes, you may find yourself upset over something of absolutely no consequence. For example, you may become terribly angered when someone cuts in front of your car in traffic. If allowed to go unchecked, this "road rage" can spread to unrelated situations and innocent people. Upon reflection, is someone else's poor driving etiquette enough reason to unleash the negative fury of your brain upon yourself and upon others? Hardly. Instead of working yourself into a frenzy, use rational, reality-based thinking. Talk to yourself like you would talk to a friend who found himself in the same situation. After a few minutes, you'll calm down.

Sometimes, of course, the problems you face are far more serious than the inconsiderate driving habits of some frustrated stranger.

From time to time, you will encounter life-altering events that leave you confused, fearful and deeply hurt. When you face such situations, remember that the more severe the problem, the greater the need for clear-headed, no-nonsense, old-fashioned common sense.

Life presents each of us with a series of situations that test our ability to think rationally. During these tough times, we are tempted to indulge in unproductive emotions such as blame, anger, sadness or guilt. These emotions almost always do more harm than good. So when life throws you a curveball, remember that you possess, free and clear, a tool that can solve your problems — if you let it. That tool is the human brain.

Resolve to make your brain a powerful problem-solving machine. Treat it as a "power tool" in the truest sense. Respect it, care for it and use it wisely. If you do, there's absolutely no end to the things you can fix.

Waiting for Godot

While we are waiting,
life passes us by.

Seneca
Roman Philosopher and Playwright
1st Century A.D.

In college, I saw a play called *Waiting for Godot*. Attendance at the play was not optional (thus explaining my presence). My classmates and I were compelled to attend by a professor whose idea of a good time was a late-night poetry reading. The play wasn't simply bad — it was torture. *Waiting for Godot* was one of those highly-regarded literary works that critics loved and the rest of us didn't understand. Especially me.

As the curtain went up, the audience was treated to a couple of guys standing around on the barren stage, waiting for some fellow named Godot. Who was Godot? They never really said. Why were they waiting? Your guess was as good as mine. When did they expect him to show up? Any minute, except that Godot was always running a little late. So I spent an entire evening watching two actors argue, whine, complain, and — above all — wait. After two hours of nonstop moaning and groaning, the curtain dropped.

P.S. ... Godot never showed.

The next day, our professor informed us that the offending playwright, a man named Samuel Beckett, had received the Nobel Prize for Literature in 1969. All I could say was that nobody had asked me for my vote.

Over the years, I've thought a lot about that crazy play, and I have a confession to make: I've mellowed. It's taken over twenty years to realize that I'm glad I went to see *Waiting for Godot*. Finally, I think I understand what Beckett was trying to say. The intervening years have shown me that all of us do a little waiting for Godot. From time to time, all of us sit around and do nothing but complain. And wait. During these times, we secretly hope that someone will come along and solve all of our problems. Like the two fellows in the play, we wait and we sit and we brood and we hope for somebody or something to bail us out.

But Godot doesn't show.

Of course, things occasionally do improve on their own, but more often than not, real solutions remain elusive. No wonder. Godot, whoever he is, probably has better things to do than solve our problems. For all we know, he may even have a few problems of his own.

Never abandoning the hope that our troubles will be resolved painlessly (or that Godot will, at last, come to the rescue), we postpone action: We procrastinate, we ruminate, and we put off until tomorrow what can and should be done today.

Despite our good intentions, we lack sufficient motivation, because fear rules our thoughts. We simply feel too discouraged to try.

So we wait…
and wait…
and wait…

The solution comes when we stop waiting and start working. After all, who says that anyone, even Godot, will go out of his way to solve our problems? Who says he could, even if he wanted to?

Godot never showed up once during the whole darned play — I'll bet he hasn't shown yet. And if we wait around for tough times to get better on their own, we're really no different than those two poor fellows in the play. We're in for a long wait because:

When it comes to solving problems, working is better than waiting.

Waiting for things to improve is discouraging because we convince ourselves (wrongly) that control is out of our hands. But once we start to work, we realize that everything doesn't depend upon Godot or anyone else for that matter. It depends upon us.

If you're under the misconception that someone or something "out there" is responsible for your personal well-being, think again. Your happiness depends upon yourself. So does the quality of your spiritual life. To a surprising extent, your health depends upon your efforts. Ditto for the condition of your finances and for the quality of your relationships. The sooner you take responsibility for these things, the sooner they begin to improve. The longer you wait, the more things stay the same.

The moment you accept full responsibility for the quality of your life, you will, as a matter of course, begin searching for solutions to the things that trouble you. When you do, there is no time left to worry about Godot's shortcomings. In fact, you'll be so busy doing *your* job that it won't occur to you to blame him or anybody else. Besides, those two fellows in the play have already done enough blaming and complaining to last two lifetimes.

Do you have a problem that cries out for a solution? Are you discouraged or afraid? Have you been postponing the inevitable, wishing that things would simply "fix themselves"? If so, it's time to stop waiting. Even if you feel uncomfortable, get busy and go to work. Despite the anxiety, face your problems head-on. Even if you are discouraged, keep trying. When you do, you'll quickly discover that working on solutions is always better than dwelling on problems.

Once you go to work, you'll have the comfort of knowing you are intensely involved in your own solutions. And that's how it should be. After all, who's got more at stake, you or Godot?

So don't wait for Godot to sweep in and fix

everything. Just get busy, go to work, and see what happens. Even if the job seems overwhelming at first, get started. One small step is an important beginning.

I've decided if I ever have the free time, I'm going to write a play of my own — my response to Beckett. I'll call it *Stopped Waiting for Godot*. My play won't require actors, and it certainly won't take two hours to perform. In fact, all that I'll need is a giant yellow post-it note, about ten feet by ten feet; if I have a big budget, I might even build a huge refrigerator door to stick it on.

As the curtain goes up, the audience will view a handwritten message on the note. That message will read: "Dear Godot, I got tired of waiting, so I decided to do it myself. Have a nice day." Who knows, I might even win a Nobel Prize.

The Two Most Tiring Days

Real generosity toward the future consists in giving all to what is present.

Albert Camus
French Philosopher, Novelist,
and Dramatist
1913 – 1960

If you're facing tough times, you're probably tired. Tough times have a way of leaving you exhausted before the day has even begun. The weariness comes not from physical labor but from constant worry. That's why it's so important to understand the source of your energy drain. Your fatigue results not from physical strain but, instead, from your attitude toward the two most tiring days of the week: yesterday and tomorrow.

Why are yesterday and tomorrow so draining? These two days represent those two limitless reservoirs of exhaustion: the past and the future. If we could simply concern ourselves with the day at hand, life would become much simpler. But sometimes we lack both the ability to accept the past and the faith to accept the future. As if today's tasks weren't enough, we take on the burdens of yesterday and the obligations of tomorrow. When we do, today's work goes wanting and tomorrow's happiness is placed in jeopardy.

Interestingly, worry is a paradoxical phenomenon. For the most part, *we worry about things that we are not doing*. In fact, if we are deeply engrossed in an activity, it's impossible to agonize over it — we are simply too busy to be concerned. Herein lies the paradox: Once we begin doing the thing that we're worried about, our worries subside.

When we ruminate about the past or fret about the future, we're inviting trouble. Unknowingly, we turn the spotlight upon ourselves, and in doing so, concoct unrealistic beliefs about the way others see us. We mistakenly convince ourselves that we're the center of everyone's attention; we come to believe that our problems and shortcomings are, to the world, what the iceberg was to the Titanic. Nothing could be further from the truth. In reality, our personal curveballs are, more often than not, far less important than the lessons we learn from them. And, ironically enough, the attitudes we hold toward our personal deficiencies are far more important than the deficiencies themselves.

If you wish to overcome perceived short-comings and feel better about your life, become engrossed in meaningful, enjoyable work. Find a productive way to occupy your time, and you'll soon discover that your spirits will begin to rise.

As soon as you become involved in today's work, your anxiety will evaporate into thin air. As you let the past and the future fend for them-selves, you will begin to live in the precious present, and you will be freed to use yesterday and tomorrow as they were intended.

So how are your yesterdays best put to use? Yesterdays are custom-made learning tools. Stored away in your personal history are powerful lessons for improving your life today. All too often, these lessons go unnoticed.

By carefully examining the important events and milestones in your life, you will come to understand the styles and patterns of be-havior that make you who you are. Sometimes, these patterns are productive — sometimes they are not.

Most of us possess the natural tendency to repeat the same old mistakes over and over again, often without realizing that today's prob-lems are simply a variation on yesterday's. Our patterns of behavior are, by their very nature, habit-forming. Left unchecked, old habits die when we do. Herein lies the value of yesterday.

If we are wise enough to look back upon yesterday with objectivity, we begin to see a clearer picture of the behaviors that worked for us in the past and those that didn't. And, because we are insightful human beings, we can make changes as needed.

If we seek to improve our lives, we must discover ways to eliminate those behaviors that hold us back while we make habits of those actions that propel us forward. Thus, the great value of yesterday is that it serves as a personal history book, one that is full of invaluable life- lessons.

Over the long run, the world tends to reward us in approximate proportion to the contributions we make. By carefully examining the past, we are able to find ways to increase our contributions to a world that desperately needs our services.

As for the future, please recognize that tomorrows are best used for planning. By taking time to plan the future, we improve the chances of getting what we want from life. But many of us are not at all sure what it is that we want or, for that matter, how we plan to get it.

Your first step in planning for tomorrow is straightforward: *Decide what you want from life*. Make this decision carefully, because once you decide upon a single, overriding goal, you are likely to achieve it.

You'll find it helpful to write you goal down on paper, but once your goal is clearly established, don't spent too much time worrying about it. Instead, follow the instructions that are so beautifully expressed in the sixth chapter of Matthew: Don't worry about tomorrow. Instead, resolve to do your best today, and then let events transpire as they will.

If you can learn from yesterday without undue regret, you are insightful. If you can plan for tomorrow without worry, you are wise. If you can live your life in one-day packages, you are blessed.

When you live in the present, there's little to worry about anyway. After all, the present is a very small sliver of time, suddenly upon us and too quickly gone. The present moment is too precious to waste but never long enough to worry about. So don't trouble yourself with those two terrible days, yesterday and tomorrow. Live to the fullest in the *only* day of the rest of your life — today.

Beyond Blame

*The fault, dear Brutus,
is not in our stars
but in ourselves....*

Shakespeare
1564–1616

In seventh grade, I studied English under a woman named Mrs. June Bowen. Mrs. Bowen had a stern look that let you know she was all business. Her appearance was neat yet proper. She was polite and respectful to students, but she could never be confused with a stand-up comedienne: no kidding around, no funny stories, no practical jokes — just English and lots of it.

In June Bowen's class, margins had to be just so; spelling mistakes were harshly graded down; punctuation was carefully monitored. Students who obeyed the rules of Mrs. Bowen and the rules of proper English experienced no problems, but woe to those who turned in sloppy work. Mrs. Bowen showed no remorse as she flunked lazy students; she expressed no trace of sadness as she handed back failing papers full of red ink.

Mrs. Bowen and I didn't see eye-to-eye, and my grades showed it. I preferred to punctuate in my own way; I spelled as the spirit moved me; and I completed assignments on my own timetable. My life would have been much improved had I simply finished my work on time, but I found it impossible to concentrate on English. As failing grades began to accumulate on my report card, I became more and more anxious. Finally, I developed a total aversion to the study of the English language. So instead of working harder, I did the natural thing.

I blamed Mrs. Bowen.

I told myself that her teaching skills were deficient (they weren't). I believed her expectations were unrealistic (they weren't). And I told any willing ear that she was terribly unfair (she wasn't). Because of my anger, I convinced myself that Mrs. Bowen was too hard, too strict, and too inflexible. Finally, I decided that she simply didn't like me. In later years, I learned that Mrs. Bowen was actually quite fond of me — it was my work she didn't like.

As the school year dragged on like a long bad dream, I became absolutely convinced that

I would fail English. But somehow, either by a miracle from God or by the mercy of June Bowen, I escaped her class with a final grade of "D." Not surprisingly, every English class after hers became a little easier. She taught English, and she taught discipline; I needed lessons in both. Today, I appreciate Mrs. Bowen, respect her, and remember her fondly.

But in seventh grade, I blamed Mrs. Bowen for my problems since she was the one handing out the failing grades. Obviously, the problem was mine, not hers, but I couldn't face my own shortcomings. So I spent time and energy blaming the instructor when I should have been studying the text book. Such is the futility of blame.

When hard times arrive, it's easy to assign blame. We're quick to name culprits and anxious to curse them. Before we realize what's happened, we've worked ourselves into a grade-A frenzy, all for naught. Unfortunately, the energy we invest in blaming others is always wasted. The world offers no payoffs for those who collect injustices; the only reward is frustration.

Blaming others gives us fleeting satisfaction, so we usually keep a few scapegoats handy, just in case. We blame bosses, co-workers, customers, parents, teachers, spouses and even children. We may blame big government or big business. Once the blaming begins, anyone or anything is a potential target. But blaming leads only to bitterness and ignorance; we make ourselves bitter because of imagined mistreatment, and we remain ignorant of our own shortcomings. Not surprisingly, we continue to make the same old mistakes — over and over.

Sometimes, we're innocent victims, but more often than not, we've played some role in creating our own troubles. Ironically, there is great hope in this fact. If we've helped create our own problems, we can also "un-create" them. Usually, all that's required to solve these problems is discipline. Once we decide to buckle down and get back to work, things begin to improve.

If life has been handing you some poor grades lately, concentrate on fixing things rather than affixing blame. Forgive everyone, starting with yourself. Blaming yourself for past mistakes serves no good purpose — after all, you can't change yesterday. Furthermore, there's no benefit in blaming others. Besides, they may be innocent.

Instead of looking for someone to blame, look for something to do. Instead of finding fault with others, look for lessons that apply to yourself. Instead of passing the buck, accept responsibility.

> *Instead of blaming the teacher,*
> *do the homework.*

Because blame doesn't work. And as long as we're blaming, neither do we.

The Bundle
of Sticks

It is best to do things systematically, since we are only human, and disorder is our worst enemy.

Hesiod
Greek Poet
8th Century B.C.

The first time I heard the story of the bundle of sticks, it was told to me by a Tennessee farmer. Then I heard the same story from a bank president. Finally, an expert in Eastern philosophy shared the very same tale. The number of different sources makes it difficult to assign proper credit: I'm not sure whether "the bundle of sticks" is a bit of backwoods lore, a metaphor for high finance, or a gem of wisdom from the Far East. What I do know is this: Anytime I hear the same bit of wisdom from so many different people, it's worth repeating. So here goes:

Imagine a thick bundle of sticks bound tightly together. Suppose someone asked you to break that bundle in two. If you attempted to break all the sticks at once, you'd be in trouble.

Big trouble. After hours of trying, what would you have to show for your efforts? Sore hands and a sour disposition.

Suppose, however, you tried a different tactic. Suppose you untied the bundle and proceeded to break each stick individually. This "one-at-a-time" method would be far superior since a single stick is easier to break than a whole bundle.

The moral to the story (if you haven't guessed by now) is simply this:

Your problems are like that bundle of sticks.

If you try to fix everything at once, you may fix nothing. Instead, you may undermine any chance of success, frustrating yourself in the process. When you try to solve many problems at once, it's harder to solve *any* problems. You're too overwhelmed to be effective. But breaking the work into smaller packages makes those impossible jobs possible.

Regrettably, most of us don't seem to tackle things one at a time. We want our problems solved immediately, if not sooner. When troubles arrive in bunches, we want to fix them in bunches — right now! Our impatience leads to wasted effort as we try, in vain, to break the unbreakable.

Sometimes it's difficult to untie the bundle of sticks. Our problems seem so interconnected that we can't envision ways of solving one problem without solving them all. We mistakenly tell ourselves that until *everything* is solved, *nothing* is solved. Consequently, we race from problem to problem, attempting "everything" and solving "nothing." The more we race, the more we worry, expending lots of energy but breaking no sticks.

In problem-solving, as in stick-breaking, it is best to approach things systematically — one item at a time. What's required is patience and focus. Patience is necessary because problems usually take time to develop — and to resolve. A patient attitude towards problem-solving allows us to focus our energies on one job until it is completed. With focus, *solutions* begin to come in bunches. One solution leads to another. After the first stick breaks, we gain confidence. Soon, momentum is established.

If you're trying to break a bundle of sticks that's too thick to get your arms around, pick out one problem and solve it. Remember:

One good solution is worth a thousand good intentions.

Instead of rushing from problem to problem,

take time to organize your thoughts. Put pencil to paper if necessary. Once you've established your plan, go to work with all the gusto you can muster.

If you're constantly distracted by other concerns, catch yourself in the act. Focus on the single stick that lies before you, break it, and then move onto the next. Soon, you'll have broken the entire bundle. One stick at a time.

Chock-full
of Options

On the human chessboard, all moves are possible.

Miriam Schiff

Unless you're an astronomy buff, you probably don't pay much attention to the nighttime sky. You may notice the moon, a few nearby stars, maybe a planet or two, and little more.

But if you want a breathtaking treat, step outside on a dark, clear night and take a careful look overhead. If you're far enough from city lights, the spectacle will take your breath away. In addition to the obvious stars, you'll notice a fine white dusting of more distant ones. Each one of those tiny specks is a star the size of our sun — or larger. It's an impressive sight, but that's not the half of it.

Point binoculars to the heavens and even more stars appear. Then, pause to consider that you're still viewing only a tiny fraction of our universe. In fact, you're not even seeing all the stars in our own Milky Way galaxy. And ours is only one of countless galaxies, each containing billions of stars.

The stars in the sky are literally too numerous to count. Billions of galaxies each containing billions of stars. It's been estimated that there are more galaxies than there are stars in the Milky Way. It's almost too amazing to contemplate.

What, you have every right to ask, does this little astronomy lesson have to do with the psychology of tough times?

It's all about options.

When life tosses us a curve, options seem to disappear like stars on a cloudy night. We look to the heavens but see only darkness. Although our stars are still there, we can't see them because tough times obscure the view. Despite our limited vision, countless alternatives exist.

Often, we don't recognize options because of our own inflexibility. We want things to be a certain way, and we're unwilling to look at alternatives. As long as we keep the blinders on, we're stuck.

Until we consider our options,
we have none.

But, if we allow ourselves to "get outside the box" and think creatively, choices, like stars, become almost infinite. As soon as we open our eyes, those options appear like bright-shining stars on a crystal-clear night.

If you are feeling trapped by circumstances that seem unchangeable, perhaps it's time to dust off your "mental binoculars" and start looking for new alternatives. Like an astronomer searching for undiscovered stars, your job during tough times is to search for new possibilities. Choices exist, even when you can't see them. In all likelihood, inflexibility or fear has temporarily clouded your vision. Your challenge is simple: Keep you eyes wide open, even when the sky is jet black. And keep looking upward, even when you're tempted to hang your head. If you do, your persistence and creativity will be rewarded. Sooner than you expect, you'll find yourself viewing a beautiful sky — that's chock-full of options.

A Presidential Prescription for Embarrassment

*T*ime is a great physician.

Benjamin Disraeli
English Statesman
1804 - 1881

The night President Nixon resigned, I was singing country music. During my brief musical career, I was never confused with Hank Williams, and our band never made it to the top — or, for that matter, the bottom — of the charts. In fact, our greatest brush with fame came during an extended summer engagement at the Holiday Inn in Stark, Florida.

Although Stark was not the nation's most glamorous musical venue, no one in the band complained. We were four college guys having a good time earning money doing something we loved. But one man wasn't having nearly as much fun that summer as we were: the president.

In the summer of '74, President Nixon found himself in deep trouble over a scandal dubbed "Watergate." Very intelligent people, including

Nixon himself, had done outrageous things that ultimately resulted in the first resignation of a United States president. Our band happened to be playing music on the night he resigned, and we couldn't resist watching a little piece of history. So on that balmy August evening, we carefully timed our first break to coincide with Nixon's momentous announcement. When the music stopped, we rushed back to the motel room and turned on the television set. The president, with a bleach-white pallor, was saying good-bye.

Watching the whole spectacle on television, I couldn't help feeling sorry for Mr. Nixon. Here was a bright and successful guy who had committed a colossal blunder, and now he had to admit his mistakes in front of the whole world. What an embarrassing moment!

After Nixon finished his speech, the band members and I returned to the lounge to begin our second set. The room was still smoky; waitresses were still serving drinks; patrons were still doing the things that people do in bars. I announced that America had a new president, but nobody in the place seemed concerned. They weren't interested in long speeches or political analyses; they only wanted to hear country music. Someone in the crowd yelled,

"Play *The Tennessee Waltz!*" and that was that. Back to twanging guitars.

So much for history in the making.

The night Mr. Nixon resigned, I learned a very valuable lesson about life's embarrassing moments: No matter how big the problem, life is bigger. Even the demise of a president doesn't change things for long. News bulletins may flash and pundits may pontificate...for awhile. But soon, people return to their activities and start thinking about more important things in life — things like *The Tennessee Waltz*.

Like Mr. Nixon, all of us find ourselves in embarrassing situations from time to time. And like Mr. Nixon, we hate to have our imperfections made public. After all, we live in a society that idealizes success and prosperity. Hard times translate into embarrassing circumstances (like job loss, bankruptcy, or divorce). In spite of the old adage about sticks and stones, public embarrassment still hurts. For most of us, the greatest pain of all comes when our troubles are made public.

I've sometimes wondered if Nixon would have been bothered by his resignation if he could have resigned in private. After all, that job paid much less than Mr. Nixon would have earned as a high-priced lobbyist in some big-time Washington law firm. Plus, think of all the troubles that go along with being president: You're constantly hounded by people looking for handouts, your appointment calendar is always full, and your every move is placed under a microscope. Who needs those kinds of headaches?

Considering the nature of a president's job, I'm convinced that Mr. Nixon might have gladly given two weeks notice, if he could have done so in private. But, the most powerful man in the world doesn't have that option; he couldn't simply clean out his desk and drift quietly into the night. Mr. Nixon, to put it succinctly, was stuck.

Some of us, like Nixon, are stuck doing things that we don't enjoy, but we're too embarrassed to call it quits. So we work in frustration for years, waiting for improvements that never come. Our procrastination speaks volumes about the power of peer pressure. Many of us are controlled not by our own wishes but by the fear of what others might think.

If you're feeling tyrannized by the opinions of others, remember that almost nobody cares as much as you think they do. No matter how big your problem may seem to you, it's probably not very big to the rest of the world. You may imagine that you're at the center of everyone's thoughts. You're not. Your mountain, like it or not, is your neighbor's molehill.

It's not that people are insensitive — it's just that when it comes to troubles, everybody has their own, so yours naturally get second billing. Even a presidential predicament cannot hold peoples' attention for long. And if a president's problems aren't worth fretting over, what does that say about all of the things that worry the rest of us?

Certainly Mr. Nixon was embarrassed for a while; he even took an extended vacation, but he didn't turn himself into a lifelong hermit. Neither should you. No problem is that big.

Epilogue

One evening, almost two decades after Watergate, I was clicking through the TV channels, and there he was: Nixon — the man who experienced so much pain on that hot August night back in 1974. Looking calm, wise and self-assured, Mr. Nixon was talking about global affairs and making lots of sense. Even a few of his enemies must have begrudgingly admired the way he rebounded from his tough times. Nixon wrote several best-selling books and became a highly respected expert on foreign affairs — all after Watergate. Plus, he wasn't afraid to appear on television and face some tough questions.

What guts! It is a small wonder that the man made such a noteworthy comeback.

For generations to come, historians will debate Nixon's life, his losses and his lessons. Some will remember President Nixon as the fellow who led us out of Vietnam and opened up trade with China, good works to be sure. Others may choose to remember him for his mistakes and his downfall. But not me. I'll remember him for the lesson he taught me about life's embarrassing moments. Because whenever I think of Mr. Nixon, one thing still comes to mind ...*The Tennessee Waltz*.

The Magic of Encouragement

A *friend is a present*
you give yourself.

R. L. Stevenson
Scottish Poet, Novelist, and Essayist
1850 - 1894

As a kid, I was a San Francisco Giants fan. In those days, a guy's favorite player was either Willie Mays or Mickey Mantle. I liked Mays, so the Giants were my favorite team. That's why I've always been a little sad that I wasn't old enough to witness the most wonderful moment in Giants' history.

It was 1951, the Giants were still playing in New York, Truman was president, and Willie Mays was a fresh-faced rookie. The National League season ended in a tie for first place, which meant a playoff was needed to determine the champion.

It was the bottom of the ninth inning of the final game, with the Giants trailing their perennial arch-rival, the Brooklyn Dodgers, by a score of 4–2. The championship was on the line, and all across the country, fans sat spellbound by their radios as Bobby Thomson came to the plate. With runners on second and third, Dodgers' pitcher Ralph Branca knew all too well that Thomson represented the winning run.

On Branca's second pitch, Thomson connected. Everyone in the park heard that familiar crack as they saw the ball leap from the bat. Back. Way back! Home run! Amid the chaos, Giants' broadcaster Russ Hodges erupted with his timeless declaration: "The Giants win the pennant! The Giants win the pennant! The Giants win the pennant ...."

Bobby Thomson circled the bases and was mobbed at home plate by fans and teammates in one of the singular moments in baseball history. Think of the satisfaction. Imagine the excitement, the thrill, the joy.

But imagine, for a moment, how Branca felt.

From time to time, all of us feel like Ralph Branca must have felt as Bobby Thomson did his home run trot on that fateful day back in 1951. We make a mistake, and it costs us. Certainly our misfortunes are seldom as public as Branca's, but they hurt just the same.

When we hit the game-winning home run, friends and fans stand at home plate ready and waiting to share in the triumph. But, when tough times arrive, there are no ticker-tape parades, no joyous celebrations. After the game is lost, many of us prefer to close ourselves off from family, friends and teammates; to do so is a mistake. In the losing locker room, we need all the encouragement we can get.

If you wish to beat Old Man Trouble at his own game, it's simply not enough to accept the encouragement of family and friends. Acceptance is a passive activity; what's called for is not passivity, but action. Instead of waiting for encouragement to find you, it's your job to find it. Once you find the right kind of support, tough times are easier to handle.

Sometimes, encouraging friends simply show up on the doorstep, willing to help. Your job is to invite them in. Other times, it seems as though you haven't a friend in the world. On those occasions, it's up to you to go out and prove yourself wrong.

Encouragement can be a ticket out of tough times, but beware: There are two kinds of encouragement, real and imitation. Real encouragement leaves you believing that you possess the strength to solve your own problems. It lifts you up, making self-pity impossible. Encouraging friends may suffer with you, but they will never pity you. Instead, they will be quick to remind you of your strengths, your options, and your resources.

After talking with encouraging friends, you will feel invigorated. You'll possess a faith that will soon translate into action. Your faith is not foolish optimism; it's a realistic assessment of your abilities.

But all encouragement is not created equal. Sometimes, encouragement is actually discouragement in disguise. On the surface, the words you hear seem helpful, but in truth, they leave you less sure of yourself than before you heard them. Sometimes, this discouragement masks itself as pity. Other times, the message concerns the misfortune of another poor soul whose trouble is even greater than your own.

Friends who pity you may mean well, but they do harm. They leave you with feelings of weakness and dread. Their message is usually a reflection of their own insecurities. *They* feel uneasy and, before long, so do you. Such conversations leave you disheartened about the future. The unspoken message is as follows: "Poor pitiful you. You're unlucky, mistreated, and helpless." This message is false advertising and contrary to your best interests.

Some of the most discouraging people in the world are genuinely well-meaning. They don't intend to make you abandon all hope, but they do so with remarkable regularity. To avoid feeling gloomy and not knowing why, avoid the gossips, the pessimists, and the self-righteous. Don't listen to the whiners who think things are hopelessly unfair. And ignore the nay-sayers who believe that mistakes are impossible to repair.

Distinguish between discouraging and encouraging friends, and start spending time with the right crowd. After all, who really needed an encouraging pal on that day back in '51, Bobby Thomson or Ralph Branca? And what kind of friends do you really need today?

Too Many
Coat Hangers

The cost of a thing is the amount of life which is required in exchange for it.

Henry David Thoreau
American Essayist and Novelist
1817 - 1862

Coat hangers are a wonderful invention: They don't cost much; they're universally available; and they almost never wear out. How many products can claim that?

Yes, coat hangers are terrific — until you acquire more than you need. Then, they create chaos in the closet. If your closet becomes overloaded with unused hangers, you've created a haberdasher's nightmare. Extra coat hangers become tangled up in everything. Before long, you're spending more time untangling hangers than you are selecting your wardrobe.

Most things in life are like coat hangers. There's a right amount, and there's too much. Find the right amount, and life becomes a little easier. Become overloaded, and you've got a mess on your hands.

We live in a society that assumes more is better. No wonder. Every day we are bombarded with advertising that tempts us to buy newer, more expensive gadgets to replace the older, less expensive ones we bought last year. Beautiful young models sell everything from soap suds to six-packs. The messages are subtle but powerful: Buy what they're selling and enjoy the good life. Even though we know better, we fall for the sales pitch time and again.

Our misguided desires for "more" can bring on tough times. Sometimes, we overspend. Other times, we create our own misery by over-committing our time or our personal resources. When we do, we pay a price by creating a messy, tangled web of problems that resembles a closet filled-to-overflowing with coat hangers. Then, there remains only one intelligent course of action: simplification.

The advantages of simplicity are seldom promoted for one important reason: Nobody has yet found a way to earn a profit by selling those advantages. You'll never hear a celebrity's paid endorsement for simplicity. And you'll never gaze into the eyes of a gorgeous spokesmodel who asks you to slow down, stop spending, and pare down your life-style.

Fortunately, there have been many wise men and women throughout history who *did* champion the simple life: Thoreau, Mother Teresa, and the man from Galilee, to name a few. But their voices are often drowned out by the din of commercialism. Consequently, we live in a world where simplicity is hard to find and even harder to keep.

That's why it's important to be able to say "no." Until you learn to say "no" to things you don't need, you're asking for trouble. But the minute you begin to reject all the excess baggage that's been pressing you down, you'll feel a great weight lifted from your shoulders.

If you've gone through a life-changing experience that left you with fewer earthly possessions, look upon it as an opportunity to simplify, and say a word of thanks. If you're working 60 hours a week in order to pay for things that you don't have time to enjoy, do whatever it takes to stop the merry-go-round. Cut up the credit cards, put yourself on a budget, and begin to exercise more self-control. Learn to say "no" to the slick salesmen who would sell you things you don't really want and certainly don't need. Learn to say "no" to yourself when you feel the urge to "treat" yourself to another shopping spree. As you learn to live with less, you'll enjoy yourself more.

Once you begin to simplify, you'll wonder why you ever wanted it any other way. You'll also learn an important lesson about life: too many hangers don't ensure a happy closet.

They prevent it.

The Dropped Pass

My life has been nothing
but a failure.

Claude Monet
French Impressionist Painter
1840-1926

Have you ever made a mistake in front of a big crowd? Unless you're a hermit, you probably have. If so, you know that sick, sinking feeling that usually accompanies public failure. And you'll understand how I felt on a terrible day back in 1963.

It was November 22, the same day that President Kennedy was assassinated. I was a nine-year-old boy playing grade-school football. That afternoon, our team met a nearby rival in a game that, to me, seemed historic.

The other team's biggest weapon was a speedster named Jimmy Elrod. Elrod was little, fast, and tough — a touchdown threat any time he handled the ball. We knew we had to stop Jimmy if we were to have any chance of winning the game.

Our team's star was quarterback Mike Regan. Big Mike was an accurate passer with a strong arm, so it was no surprise when we scored first on a long bomb — Regan to me. Seven zip. Unfortunately, our team didn't hold the lead for long.

Elrod answered with two quick touchdowns. After missing both extra points, they still led 12 to 7. That's the way it stayed until late in the game.

With almost no time left on the clock, our squad was closing in on a touchdown when Mike called my number. If I made the catch, we'd win the game. If I dropped the pass, the game would be over ... and we would lose.

Regan yelled "Hike!" and I took off into an open area safely behind enemy lines. Thirty years have passed, but I can still see the perfect spiral on the ball as it left Mike's hand in apparent slow motion. I can still hear the hush of the crowd, and I can still feel the texture of the pigskin as it lightly touched my fingertips.

And I can still sense my stunned horror as the ball brushed past my fingers and fell to the ground. Incomplete pass. The game was over, we lost, and I felt like a complete failure.

Looking back on that day back in 1963, it is now easy to put things in perspective. As an adult, I know that fourth-grade sporting events are not the "end-all" and "be-all" of life. Childhood games are not nearly as important as they seem to nine-year-old boys. In truth, I was never really a "failure" for dropping the ball. I was simply a little boy trying hard — maybe too hard.

When a child labels himself a failure, we are quick to correct him, and rightfully so. But when grown-ups make mistakes, the labeling sticks. We adults take winning and losing very seriously. If we suffer painful losses in business, marriage, or finance, we feel like failures — we may even brand ourselves as such.

We beat ourselves up. We live with self-sabotaging guilt that is undeserved. By labeling ourselves as "failures," we create negative attitudes that are difficult to exorcise.

When I think back to that '63 football season, I realize that no other person on earth remembers that game in the same way that I do. No one has a vivid memory of the dropped pass — no one, that is, but me. That pass was important to me and nobody else. Was I a failure? Only in my own mind.

As adults, all of us drop an occasional pass: Mistakes are simply the price we pay for playing the game. In fact, mistakes are not only inevitable, they can also be *helpful,* because they have the power to teach us lessons that we could learn in no other way. Once mistakes are made, the strategy for rational adults is simple: Learn from those mistakes and move on.

Instead of feeling sorry for ourselves, or embarrassed, we should vow to improve. Instead of quitting the team, we should ask the coach to put us back in — as soon as possible. After all, there are still lots of passes to catch and plenty more touchdowns to score — just as long as we keep playing the game.

Sad About Cris

Sadness flies on the wings of morning, and out of darkness comes the light.

Jean Giraudoux
French Dramatist, Novelist, and Diplomat
1882 - 1944

When Cris died, he was nine and I was seven. Cris was my dog, a feisty little black-and-white mutt, one of the cutest dogs you ever saw. To seven-year-old boys, dogs are a lot like people, and Cris was no exception. He was more like a brother than a pet. We grew up together, played together, even slept in the same bed (when Mom wasn't looking). So it was no surprise that the news hit hard when they called to say that Cris had been hit by a car and killed.

That night, when I returned home from my grandmother's, I wasn't the only one crying. The whole family was overcome. My parents had adopted Cris from the pound two years before their first baby arrived. He was a full-fledged member of the family, and the loss was a terrible blow.

A kind neighbor had already taken the body to the local animal shelter, so I never saw Cris again. Ever. But my father did a very wise thing that made the pain a little easier to take.

He had a funeral.

It wasn't a "real" funeral because the earthly remains were long since gone, but that fact didn't matter to us. Our family held hands, cried, talked about Cris, and said a prayer. Somehow, that little service made the loss easier to accept.

Funerals serve a purpose. They give us time to feel our loss and express our sadness. By doing so, we move through the process of grieving, eventually moving forward with our lives. When people die, we're accustomed to funerals. But when it comes to other losses, we sometimes forget to bury the dead.

Thirty years after Cris died, I faced a different kind of loss: the loss of my business. Ours had been a family-owned real estate operation founded by my grandfather nine years before I was born. Economic forces drove the company into a merger with a local competitor — for me, this was a painful loss. I was left to close up shop.

What a terrible time in my life: I suffered sleepless nights, crushing stress, and untold guilt. As business activities wound to a close, I was preoccupied with bankers, lawyers, and employees. A funeral was the furthest thing from my mind.

Several years passed. Eventually, I left the field of real estate altogether and moved to Chicago to pursue a doctorate in clinical psychology. Still, the loss of my business haunted me at every turn. One day I was sitting in a classroom listening to a noted psychologist give a lecture on the subject of grieving, and suddenly it hit me.

It was time for another funeral.

Upon my return to Nashville, I headed straight for my old office building — by now, any trace of the family business was gone. A carpet company had moved in on the ground floor. An insurance salesman was working in my old office. An engineering firm had taken up residence in space once used by our accounting department. Things were certainly different now, but that wasn't important.

I stood in the parking lot, looking at surroundings that had once been so very familiar. And I had a private service.

We live in a society that doesn't often take sufficient time to heal its wounds. When we lose things of great importance, we're often encouraged to go about our business as though nothing had happened. We simply don't take enough time to feel the loss...and to heal.

If something in your life needs burying, bury it. Whether it's a former job, a broken relationship or a shattered dream, your loss needs to be mourned. Have a funeral. If you feel comfortable, invite family and friends. If not, do it by yourself. Even if the loss is a very old one, be willing to pay your respects.

Because funerals serve a purpose.

And it's never too late for a private service.

Faith in the Lost-and-Found

Without faith,
nothing is possible.
With it, nothing
is impossible.

Mary McLeod Bethune
American Educator

In kindergarten we had a "lost-and-found" box. It was a simple cardboard box adorned with colored construction paper. Whenever something of value was misplaced, the teacher pointed to that little box and, sure enough, the lost item was usually there.

Did you lose a mitten? Look in the lost-and-found. Missing the scarf your mother knitted? Ditto. Lost that fat pencil or your favorite pair of scissors? Go check the lost-and-found.

The lost-and-found box never contained great material riches. If you were searching for bundles of cash, diamonds or jewels, you must look elsewhere. But if you wanted to retrieve something personal — something that was uniquely yours — the lost-and-found was the place to go.

In life, as in kindergarten, it's easy to lose things. But grown-up losses can be much more painful than disappearing scarves or unclaimed mittens. Grown-ups can lose wealth, prestige, even health. These hurts are troublesome ... sometimes devastating. But the greatest loss of all has nothing to do with earthly possessions. It has to do with faith.

When life takes a sharp turn for the worse, it's easy to lose faith. We lose faith in ourselves. We lose faith in the future. We lose faith in other people. We may even lose faith in God. Amidst the confusion, we may stray from trusted sources of spiritual strength. It's not that we do so intentionally. It's just that we're faced with so many unanswered questions. We can't seem to find time for something as esoteric as faith. After all, there are things to be done, bills to be paid, and worries to be worried.

As hope slips through the cracks, a new belief system replaces the old. We come to believe the worst. We lose confidence in the future; we see no meaning for our lives; and we sometimes sink into the darkness of depression.

Depression is negative faith. It is the expectation of a future without joy. It is belief in a world without hope. It is the firm conviction that life cannot be repaired. Sometimes depression has its origin in physical causes — the obvious cure is medicine. But many times, this profound sadness stems from a crisis of personal faith, so a different prescription is called for.

If you've recently faced a life-changing disappointment, your faith may be in short supply. If so, it's possible that you're asking yourself the wrong questions. You may be asking "Why me?" when you should be asking "What now?" When you ask "Why me?", you concentrate on the unfairness of your personal situation. As long as you remain stuck in the "Why me?" mode, you focus your thoughts and emotions on yesterday's disappointments. But when you ask "What now?", you focus your energies on the things you *can* do, not the things you can't.

The sooner you can move from "Why me?" to "What now?", the sooner you'll begin to move beyond tough times. And the sooner you'll plant the seeds of spiritual renewal. Of course, your spiritual renewal is a personal matter. It may include daily quiet time, a time for prayer and regular worship. You may find renewal in the silent beauty of a sunrise or the blooming of a flower. Wherever you find your strength, go there often. And when life takes a turn for the worse, be sure to peek into your spiritual lost-

and-found box. Your faith may not look exactly like mine or like your neighbor's, and that's okay. Look for the faith that is genuinely yours, and when you find it, hold on tight.

Even when you feel that God is very far away, even when you fear that your faith will be lost forever, don't despair. Know that your faith has not been destroyed, it's only been hidden from view. Once you decide to search for it, you won't have to look very far.

Spiritual health is a powerful gift you can give yourself. When you're ready to ask the right questions, spiritual treasures await. Those treasures are yours — and they're safely tucked away very nearby. So why not claim them now?

Perspective in a Cemetery

The present will not long endure.

Pindar
Greek Poet
4th Century B.C.

When life hands us unexpected troubles, small problems begin to assume enormous proportions. Times of crisis make it difficult for us to maintain perspective. Instead of thinking things through rationally, we allow ourselves to be swept away by the emotions of the moment. This sort of panic psychology is contagious; it spreads through marriages, families, schools and businesses like an infectious disease (which, in a way, it is). If we are to live happy, healthy lives, panic thinking must be stopped before it infects us and the people we love.

When the concerns of the day seem overwhelming and insoluble, we need a quiet place to go to put things back into perspective. We desperately need an island of sanity amid the sea of turmoil. That place, surprisingly enough, is the cemetery. Any cemetery.

And what, you ask, could possibly be up-lifting about a graveyard? Just this: Graveyards and tombstones serve to remind us that, in fewer days than we might like, this earthly journey will be over. The sadness we are feeling will be gone; our worries will be gone; our wounds will be healed. The problems that seem so troubling today will, in time, vanish into thin air like the morning dew. An occasional visit to the cemetery reminds us that no earthly problems are permanent. By remembering this fact, we observe the ironclad rule for overcoming tough times — we keep things in proper perspective.

Perspective is a scarce commodity because we humans have great difficulty distinguishing between big problems and little ones. We allow minor inconveniences to upset us; we permit insignificant problems to influence our moods; we waste valuable time and energy fretting over things that don't deserve to be fretted over. In short, we lose perspective, and we pay a very dear price for that loss. In the absence of perspective, we fail to realize that most of our problems are, in reality, little problems.

Without perspective, we take little troubles and blow them into big ones. Money becomes a big problem. Work becomes a big problem. The opinions of others assume great importance. We take any of a thousand nuisances and convince ourselves that they are big, important, all-consuming problems. But they're not — unless, that is, we make them big, important, all-consuming problems by exaggerating their significance.

And how can we sort out the little problems from big ones? Here's a simple, foolproof method for determining the relative importance of the troubles that each of us face: *Big problems concern health and freedom. Everything else is a little problem.*

Health problems come in at least three flavors: spiritual, physical, and psychological. A serious deficit in any of these areas will, if left unattended, bear bitter fruit. Health problems should, therefore, always be considered serious until proven otherwise. Health concerns are not, under any circumstances, to be ignored, postponed or swept under the rug.

As for the matter of personal freedom, this, too, is an area of vital concern for every human being. Issues relating to freedom can be grouped into at least two categories: physical and emotional. If one loses the ability to move freely within society, this loss of physical freedom is a grave insult to the human spirit, a serious problem to be sure.

Individuals who adopt an overly dependent style of living forfeit their emotional freedom; this, too, qualifies as a big problem. Those people who, in the absence of serious health problems, become totally dependent on others do themselves a severe disservice. Interdependency in human affairs is both appropriate and healthy; total or near-total dependency, on the other hand, is a serious problem that should be addressed without delay.

As long as you and your loved ones possess the gifts of health and freedom, consider yourselves lucky. And consider your problems small ones. Then, pledge to yourself that you will never again worry about small problems. Ever.

Most problems that concern us can be categorized as "small," "very small," or "tiny." We worry about a bigger house, a newer car or a quicker promotion. We worry about things that our neighbors are saying. We worry about things we can't control and things we cannot change. We worry about savings accounts, income taxes, and mortgage balances — little problems all.

Worrying too much about little problems, ironically enough, creates big ones. When we lose perspective and focus inordinate amounts of energy on little problems, we invite unwelcome side effects like anxiety and depression. Anxiety and depression ultimately manifest themselves through physical illness (creating big problems). In such cases, we allow our attitudes toward insignificant issues to cause significant suffering.

For many of us, perspective comes only after hardship or loss. Until our spirits are shaken to their very foundations, we find ourselves dwelling on minor inconveniences. That's why it's helpful to find perspective in a cemetery.

Standing amid the graves of those who have gone before, we gain a healthy dose of reality. If we're attentive, voices from beyond the tombstones have much to tell. They instruct us to look at the rose instead of the thorn. They ask us to think less of ourselves and more of others. They challenge us to walk through the world with our eyes and hearts open.

So the next time you're faced with tough times, ask yourself if this problem will concern you on your deathbed. If not, don't disturb yourself too much.

Size up your problems before they ruin your day (or, for that matter, your life). Separate little ones from big ones, imagined ones from real ones, and controllable ones from un-controllable ones. Accept the ones you can't change without exaggerating the rest, and then go to work. You may be surprised. Most troubles are not as big as they first appear.

Have you got big problems? Take them to the cemetery. Have a quiet chat with the people who are resting there. And see if they can help you put things into perspective.

Little Angie and the Stolen Scissors

If you listen to your conscience, it will serve you as no other friend you'll ever know.

Loretta Young
American Actress

My wife's grandmother is named Angie Gammon Knight, but everybody in the family calls her Nanny. Nanny has plenty of stories from those childhood days she spent roaming the backwoods of Tennessee, and she's not bashful about sharing them. One of Nanny's favorites is the tale we in the family call, "Little Angie and the Stolen Scissors."

It seems that when Angie was a small girl, her family could not afford "store-bought" goods. As she recalls, "If we couldn't grow it, catch it, chop it, or sew it, we didn't own it." One day, little Angie was visiting a neighbor's house when she saw a shiny new pair of scissors. As Angie tells it, she simply didn't see how she could live without those scissors...so, against her better judgment, she decided to steal them. When the neighbor woman turned her head, Angie grabbed the scissors, stuffed them into her pocket and ran straight home.

As soon as Angie was safely inside her house, she took out the stolen prize; however, any happiness she felt was short-lived. In those days, good neighbors knew practically everything about each other. So it was no surprise when Angie's mother accurately identified the scissors as the neighbor's. Caught red-handed, Angie at first tried to lie her way out of trouble. But Mother knew better: This was a cut-and-dried case.

Immediately, Angie was made to turn around, return to the scene of the crime, hand over the stolen property, and apologize to the rightful owner. Angie said that trip to the neighbor's house was perhaps the hardest journey she ever made, but it taught her a valuable lesson that's lasted a lifetime. Angie learned that crime doesn't pay and that character counts.

Kids of every generation get themselves into mischief: They act impulsively and sometimes take things that don't belong to them. Sometimes they throw tantrums or strike out at others; sometimes they don't play fair. When kids misbehave, they eventually get caught. The same, of course, goes for grown-ups.

We grown-ups, when given half a chance, can do more mischief than a dozen kids. We do things that we know to be wrong, hoping not to get caught. But whenever we compromise our ethical standards, it's only a matter of time until justice prevails.

Character is a topic that seems, to some, a little old-fashioned. We live in a world that may look the other way in matters of conscience; we talk of "situational ethics" and "expediency." As a society, we seem reluctant to make firm pronouncements about the value and necessity of personal integrity. Thus, the line between right and wrong often becomes blurred. Although discussions of character may have become passé, the human need for a firm moral foundation is greater than ever, especially during tough times.

All too often, the chaos in our lives is caused by our own unwillingness to listen to the quiet little voice inside. Instead of following our own better judgment, we make compromises. Instead of listening to our conscience, we do the easy thing, the tempting thing, the popular thing, the expedient thing; and, like little Angie Gammon, we suffer bitter consequences.

The writer Elbert Hubbard observed, "We are punished not for our sins, but by them." Hubbard understood that crimes never go unpunished, even when we think we've escaped judgment. Life is tough enough when we behave ourselves, but when we misbehave, life becomes unmanageable. The answer to our problems, of course, lies in the vigorous application of personal integrity.

Character is the willingness to do the right thing for the right reasons at the right time, even when we'd rather do something else. Character is the compass that guides right behavior; it is the inner voice that serves as an early warning system against misconduct. Character is the yardstick by which our actions are ultimately measured. And, whether we like it or not, character is the mechanism by which all of us become fully functioning adults. Without a personal commitment to character-centered living, each of us remains childlike in our approach to life.

Once we allow a few timeless principles to guide our daily lives, decisions become easier. When we decide to do the "right" thing instead of the "easy" thing, our choices become clear. We no longer make the same old mistakes, and we no longer throw *ourselves* the same old curveballs. Which brings us back to Angie Gammon.

One day long ago, little Angie made a pledge to learn from her mistake. And she did. With the help of her mother, Angie learned a lesson for a lifetime. The scissors she stole cost, in those days, a dime. But her lesson in character-building was priceless.

The ultimate goal of life is not to possess things of value, it is to become a person of value. Each of us does so when we begin making decisions, large and small, based upon principles not preferences. Just ask Angie.

The Christmas Tie

*Life is not breath,
but action — life consists
less in length of days
than in the keen
sense of living.*

Jean-Jacques Rousseau
French Philosopher

During high school, half the boys in my class were madly in love with Lisa Elcan. Small wonder. Lisa was the kind of girl whom all boys liked; she was attractive, bright and thoughtful. To her credit, Lisa had such a big heart that even wannabe suitors (like me) could call her "friend," without resenting the fact that her real boy-friends were always tall, dark and handsome.

Unfortunately for the rest of the guys, only one man could be the lucky "Mr. Right," and that honor went to Jim Brunner, a dashing fellow who somehow convinced Lisa Elcan to become Lisa Elcan Brunner. They were married and, by rights, should have lived happily ever after. But it was not to be. Long before Lisa's fortieth birth-day, she was stricken with cancer.

If ever I needed a firsthand, living, breathing example that life is not fair, Lisa Elcan Brunner was that example. Lisa didn't deserve cancer. She was a God-fearing, hard-working young woman who dedicated herself to family and friends. She was an avid physical fitness buff and a health-food fanatic, long before the rest of us had even *heard* of tofu or bean sprouts.

Lisa was an encouraging friend, a loving wife, a caring sister and a faithful daughter. No, Lisa didn't deserve her illness, but, as we all know, life is not "fair" in the sense that mere mortals understand fairness. So Lisa became sick, and those of us who loved and admired her were left to sit and scratch our heads, wondering "Why?"

During the last year of her life, I visited Lisa whenever I could, and I was always the better for it. Somehow, she managed to remain upbeat, even when she felt extremely ill. She was an inspiration to family and friends even though her health continued to decline. As her physical strength ebbed, her spiritual strength flowed.

As fall gave way to winter that year, all of our thoughts turned to the holiday season, including Lisa's. She became very concerned about her shopping list. Confined to her bed, and with only a few months to live, Lisa managed to conduct a clandestine shopping spree with a little help from her sisters. The sisters went to stores, took careful notes, and returned home with a full report. Lisa made the final decisions. Then, her sisters returned, money in hand, to make the purchases.

My gift from Lisa that year was a red bow tie covered with tiny imprints of Santa Claus. Of course, I still wear it every Christmas. And each time I reach into my closet for that tie, I am reminded of the great lesson that Lisa taught me, not through words, but through example: You see, until the day she died, Lisa Elcan Brunner never quit living.

Life is, of course, unfair to all of us. From time to time, we receive bad breaks that we don't deserve; we lose loved ones; we suffer trials and tribulations that we didn't cause and can't understand. During these toughest of times, waves of desperation beat us down like a pounding surf. We're tempted to give up and slip beneath the tide.

But even when we feel nothing but despair, there exists within each of us the power to reclaim the gift of life and make the best of whatever time we're given. Because that time is limited, each day is priceless.

Life is short, far too short to miss out on the love and the laughter; far too short to lose hope; too short not to help others; too short not to give thanks. Life is too precious and too brief to waste a single day mired in the emotional quicksand of bitterness or regret.

Life is meant to be lived, if possible, right up until the last day: That's the lesson that Lisa Elcan Brunner taught me. And it's the reminder that she continues to share with me every time I look in the mirror and tighten the knot of my Santa Claus tie.

At some point, most of us come to the startling realization that our days on earth are numbered. Then (and only then) are we free to live each moment as a gift not to be squandered. Only when we begin to number our days are we free to choose how we will respond to the reality of a finite earthly existence: Will we really live, or will we be content to simply go through the motions?

"Going through the motions" is a mighty temptation. Life is difficult. To live honestly and authentically is more difficult still. All of us can be tempted to run for the couch, turn on the TV, and wait for the test pattern. But life beckons patiently, giving each of us countless opportunities to grow and to share our gifts with a world that desperately needs the very best we have to offer.

For all of us, fall is turning into winter. The holiday season approaches. But there remains time to live and time to share our unique gifts. When we do, we leave behind — each in his or her own way — a priceless, beautiful Christmas tie that the world will wear forever.

Filling the
Tool Box

*Man is a
tool-using animal....
Without tools,
he is nothing;
with tools, he is all.*

Thomas Carlyle
Scottish-born Author and Lecturer
1795-1881

Before returning to graduate school, I worked in and around apartment buildings. During 20 years of leasing and managing rental properties, I had the pleasure of working with hundreds of men and women who maintained and repaired all sorts of things. Among the many fine men and women I encountered, one person still stands out in my mind. That man is Alvin Wilson.

Alvin loved his work and was very good at it, laboring with the care and confidence of a skilled craftsman. For years, I consulted Alvin before hiring any new maintenance workers. In fact, I was so impressed by his judgment that I asked Alvin to sit with me as I interviewed potential applicants. Listening to Alvin, I learned an important lesson about maintenance and about life.

Alvin Wilson had an unorthodox interviewing style. Occasionally, he would ask a few technical questions, but most of his time was spent in seemingly idle conversation. Finally, at the close of the interview, Alvin would, without exception, ask the same question of each applicant:

Alvin asked to see his tool box.

In each interview, the tool-box inspection was the moment of truth. Alvin Wilson understood the importance of a good tool kit, and he understood that everybody doesn't own one. That's why Alvin never hired anybody without first getting a close look at the tools the person used to do his or her work.

If the applicant owned no tools, this was a bad sign. If the tools were broken, lost, or in disarray, Alvin was not impressed. But, if an applicant produced a well-organized and well-stocked box of tools, we'd start filling out payroll information.

In time, Alvin's theory of workmanship came to be known as "Wilson's Law." Wilson's Law, in its simplest form, states that "tools speak louder than words." Wilson's Law is more than a clever hiring strategy; it is also a guide for better living.

If we wish to rise above life's inevitable challenges, we need tools. These tools aren't found in the local hardware store; these are the ideas, the principles, the relationships, and the behaviors that, if used regularly, mold us into better people.

Without knowing it, we've been stocking our tool kits since childhood; parents, teachers, family, and friends have helped. The kit contains things like clear thinking, sincere spirituality, persistence, faith, encouraging friends and productive work. Proper rest, exercise, and diet are also important. Out tools allow us to face each new day with courage, helping us learn from our troubles and build better lives with the knowledge. The more we use the tools we've been given, the sooner we begin to make repairs.

Some of the tools we need are familiar to us while others may have become a little rusty from disuse. Furthermore, tough times may deplete our inner resources to the point that our spiritual and emotional tool kits seem almost empty. If so, it's time to restock with time-tested ideas and behaviors that work.

The essays in this book have been intended to help you reconsider which tools deserve an honored place in your kit. Hopefully, as you reclaim the spiritual and emotional tools that are, by rights, already yours, you'll be reminded of the following simple truths about tough times:

Working is better than waiting.

Fixing is better than blaming.

Your mind is more powerful than your problems.

Your outlook is critical to your success, and ...

The better your tools, the better your chances.

Your personal tool kit will probably contain a collection of books that you find helpful to your situation. Refer to them daily. You may also wish to begin keeping a journal in which you record your ideas, your insights, your goals, and your plans for the future. Such journals are invaluable history books, as well as personalized handbooks for recovery.

It is important to remember that encouraging friends and family can play an important role in your journey. Seek them out. And whatever your spiritual heritage, revisit it. When tough times arrive, God may appear to you to be far and distant. In fact, He is close at hand, waiting patiently for you to ask for His help. But ask you must.

Even during the most difficult times, countless resources are available to you, but these resources do not magically appear on your doorstep. You must do your part by organizing the tools and reaching out for the resources you need to overcome your particular difficulty. So when life tosses you a curve, remember Wilson's Law. Dust off the tools you were given as a child. You'll be surprised how well they still work, and you'll be amazed at the changes that will occur in your life.

All because you decided to pull out that old tool box — and start filling it up.

Changing the End
of the Story

*Nothing endures
but change.*

Heraclitus
Greek Philosopher
5th Century B.C.

I've heard it said that before his death the eccentric billionaire Howard Hughes liked to watch an old movie called "Ice Station Zebra." I don't know much about the movie, but I think it starred Ernest Borgnine and was a story about an outpost at the North Pole. It was rumored that Hughes watched the movie hundreds, possibly thousands, of times.

That Mr. Hughes supposedly watched videos almost every night is not unusual. Millions of people do that. What *is* unusual is that he may have watched *the same video* night after night. Watching "Ice Station Zebra" a thousand times seems crazy, since the movie never changes. I'll admit that I'm as big an Ernest Borgnine fan as the next guy, but nobody's good enough to watch every night. After all, reruns never change.

Thankfully, our lives are not like movies. We possess the power to change our stories any time we're ready. We don't have to watch "Ice Station Zebra" a thousand times; instead, we can transform our own stories while we live them.

During hard times, our stories become troubling, with no happy endings in sight. But those stories need not end in sadness. Until the final curtain closes, the ending remains unwritten. And there's always time to rewrite the script.

You're the writer, producer and star of your own story, so why not take control? Forget about blaming others. Simply rewrite your role and start the cameras rolling ...

If you don't like the scenery...
switch sets.

If you don't like your role...
become a new character.

If your supporting cast gets you down...
audition new co-stars.

If your story screams for action...
direct it.

Encouraging friends will help shoulder the load, but you must also do your part by maintaining proper perspective while working diligently on your problems. Along the way, you will acquire the maturity to avoid the traps of blame and envy. And you'll learn to overcome the unfounded worries that, in the past, led to hesitation and doubt.

Slowly at first, and then more quickly, you'll see changes. You won't repeat the same old mistakes. Instead, you'll craft a new, improved story — one that brings you pleasure and fulfillment.

So don't believe for a minute that you're trapped in a script that can't change. Your life story isn't complete. Certainly, like all of us, your story contains ups and downs. It holds successes and failures; wins and losses; joys and heartbreaks. But your life story is far from over. Like any suspenseful script, the ending is uncertain...until the final page is turned.

That ending is up to you. May yours be a joyful and triumphant conclusion.

About the Author

Criswell Freeman is a Doctor of Clinical Psychology who lives, writes and works in Nashville, Tennessee. Dr. Freeman is also the author of *The Wisdom Series* published by Walnut Grove Press. *The Wisdom Series* is a collection containing over thirty inspirational quotation books. In addition to his work as a writer, Freeman also hosts the nationally syndicated radio program *Wisdom Made in America.*

For more information about other books from Walnut Grove Press, please call 1-800-256-8584.